Go Daily with God

An Inspirational Journal
for Christians

Annie Gordon

Be strong and courageous. Do not be afraid or terrified because of them, for the Lord your God goes with you; he will never leave you nor forsake you

Deuteronomy 31:6

My name is: ....

I will go daily with the Lord my God

Fight the good fight of the faith. Take hold of the eternal life to which you were called when you made your good confession in the presence of many witnesses.

1 Timothy 6:12

This year, I promise to...

Always in my prayers ...

The LORD is my light and my salvation whom shall I fear? The LORD is the stronghold of my life— of whom shall I be afraid? When the wicked advance against me to devour me,it is my enemies and my foes who will stumble and fall.Though an army besiege me, my heart will not fear;though war break out against me,even then I will be confident.
Psalm 27 1-3

My reflections

²⁵ "Therefore I tell you, do not worry about your life, what you will eat or drink; or about your body, what you will wear. Is not life more than food, and the body more than clothes? ²⁶ Look at the birds of the air; they do not sow or reap or store away in barns, and yet your heavenly Father feeds them. Are you not much more valuable than they? ²⁷ Can any one of you by worrying add a single hour to your life. ²⁸ "And why do you worry about clothes? See how the flowers of the field grow. They do not labor or spin. ²⁹ Yet I tell you that not even Solomon in all his splendor was dressed like one of these. ³⁰ If that is how God clothes the grass of the field, which is here today and tomorrow is thrown into the fire, will he not much more clothe you—you of little faith? ³¹ So do not worry, saying, 'What shall we eat?' or 'What shall we drink?' or 'What shall we wear?' ³² For the pagans run after all these things, and your heavenly Father knows that you need them. ³³ But seek first his kingdom and his righteousness, and all these things will be given to you as well. ³⁴ Therefore do not worry about tomorrow, for tomorrow will worry about itself. Each day has enough trouble of its own.

Matthew 6:25-34

My reflections on

Matthew 6:25-34

28 Do you not know? Have you not heard? The LORD is the everlasting God, the Creator of the ends of the earth. He will not grow tired or weary, and his understanding no one can fathom.

29 He gives strength to the weary and increases the power of the weak.

30 Even youths grow tired and weary, and young men stumble and fall;

31 but those who hope in the LORD will renew their strength. They will soar on wings like eagles; they will run and not grow weary, they will walk and not be faint.

Isaiah 40:28-31

My reflections

And the God of all grace, who called you to his eternal glory in Christ, after you have suffered a little while, will himself restore you and make you strong, firm and steadfast.

1 Peter 5:10

Prayer for Today

Verse for Today

My reflections on today's verse

What Inspired Me Today

What have I been mindful of today?

Dear Lord, teach me to be

_____

_____

_____

_____

Dear Lord, share your light on

_____

_____

_____

_____

Dear Lord, hear my prayers for

_____

_____

_____

_____

Today I was grateful for...

Today I was encouraged by...

Today I saw God's hand in...

Today's Diary Notes

Prayer for Today

Verse for Today

My reflections on today's verse

What Inspired Me Today

What have I been mindful of today?

Dear Lord, teach me to be

_____

Dear Lord, share your light on

_____

Dear Lord, hear my prayers for

Today I was grateful for...

Today I was encouraged by...

Today I saw God's hand in...

Today's Diary Notes

Prayer for Today

Verse for Today

My reflections on today's verse

What Inspired Me Today

What have I been mindful of today?

Dear Lord, teach me to be

_____
_____
_____
_____

Dear Lord, share your light on

_____
_____
_____
_____

Dear Lord, hear my prayers for

_____
_____
_____
_____

Today I was grateful for...

Today I was encouraged by...

Today I saw God's hand in...

Today's Diary Notes

Prayer for Today

Verse for Today

My reflections on today's verse

What Inspired Me Today

What have I been mindful of today?

Dear Lord, teach me to be

Dear Lord, share your light on

Dear Lord, hear my prayers for

Today I was grateful for...

Today I was encouraged by...

Today I saw God's hand in...

Today's Diary Notes

Prayer for Today

Verse for Today

My reflections on today's verse

What Inspired Me Today

What have I been mindful of today?

Dear Lord, teach me to be

_____
_____
_____
_____

Dear Lord, share your light on

_____
_____
_____
_____

Dear Lord, hear my prayers for

_____
_____
_____
_____

Today I was grateful for...

Today I was encouraged by...

Today I saw God's hand in...

Today's Diary Notes

Prayer for Today

Verse for Today

My reflections on today's verse

What Inspired Me Today

What have I been mindful of today?

Dear Lord, teach me to be

Dear Lord, share your light on

Dear Lord, hear my prayers for

Today I was grateful for...

Today I was encouraged by...

Today I saw God's hand in...

Today's Diary Notes

Prayer for Today

Verse for Today

My reflections on today's verse

What Inspired Me Today

What have I been mindful of today?

Dear Lord, teach me to be

Dear Lord, share your light on

Dear Lord, hear my prayers for

Today I was grateful for...

Today I was encouraged by...

Today I saw God's hand in...

Today's Diary Notes

Prayer for Today

Verse for Today

My reflections on today's verse

What Inspired Me Today

What have I been mindful of today?

Dear Lord, teach me to be

Dear Lord, share your light on

Dear Lord, hear my prayers for

Today I was grateful for...

Today I was encouraged by...

Today I saw God's hand in...

Today's Diary Notes

Prayer for Today

Verse for Today

My reflections on today's verse

What Inspired Me Today

What have I been mindful of today?

Dear Lord, teach me to be

_____

_____

_____

_____

Dear Lord, share your light on

_____

_____

_____

_____

Dear Lord, hear my prayers for

_____

_____

_____

_____

Today I was grateful for...

Today I was encouraged by...

Today I saw God's hand in...

Today's Diary Notes

Prayer for Today

Verse for Today

My reflections on today's verse

What Inspired Me Today

What have I been mindful of today?

Dear Lord, teach me to be

Dear Lord, share your light on

Dear Lord, hear my prayers for

Today I was grateful for...

Today I was encouraged by...

Today I saw God's hand in...

Today's Diary Notes

Prayer for Today

Verse for Today

My reflections on today's verse

What Inspired Me Today

What have I been mindful of today?

Dear Lord, teach me to be

_____

_____

_____

_____

Dear Lord, share your light on

_____

_____

_____

_____

Dear Lord, hear my prayers for

_____

_____

_____

_____

Today I was grateful for...

Today I was encouraged by...

Today I saw God's hand in...

Today's Diary Notes

Prayer for Today

Verse for Today

My reflections on today's verse

What Inspired Me Today

What have I been mindful of today?

Dear Lord, teach me to be

_____

_____

_____

_____

Dear Lord, share your light on

_____

_____

_____

_____

Dear Lord, hear my prayers for

_____

_____

_____

_____

Today I was grateful for...

Today I was encouraged by...

Today I saw God's hand in...

Today's Diary Notes

Prayer for Today

Verse for Today

My reflections on today's verse

What Inspired Me Today

What have I been mindful of today?

Dear Lord, teach me to be

_____

_____

_____

_____

Dear Lord, share your light on

_____

_____

_____

_____

Dear Lord, hear my prayers for

_____

_____

_____

_____

Today I was grateful for...

Today I was encouraged by...

Today I saw God's hand in...

Today's Diary Notes

Prayer for Today

Verse for Today

My reflections on today's verse

What Inspired Me Today

What have I been mindful of today?

Dear Lord, teach me to be

_____

_____

Dear Lord, share your light on

_____

_____

Dear Lord, hear my prayers for

_____

_____

Today I was grateful for...

Today I was encouraged by...

Today I saw God's hand in...

Today's Diary Notes

Prayer for Today

Verse for Today

My reflections on today's verse

What Inspired Me Today

What have I been mindful of today?

Dear Lord, teach me to be

_____
_____
_____
_____

Dear Lord, share your light on

_____
_____
_____
_____

Dear Lord, hear my prayers for

_____
_____
_____
_____

Today I was grateful for...

Today I was encouraged by...

Today I saw God's hand in...

Today's Diary Notes

Prayer for Today

Verse for Today

My reflections on today's verse

What Inspired Me Today

What have I been mindful of today?

Dear Lord, teach me to be

_____

_____

_____

_____

Dear Lord, share your light on

_____

_____

_____

_____

Dear Lord, hear my prayers for

_____

_____

_____

_____

Today I was grateful for...

Today I was encouraged by...

Today I saw God's hand in...

Today's Diary Notes

Prayer for Today

Verse for Today

My reflections on today's verse

What Inspired Me Today

What have I been mindful of today?

Dear Lord, teach me to be

Dear Lord, share your light on

Dear Lord, hear my prayers for

Today I was grateful for...

Today I was encouraged by...

Today I saw God's hand in...

Today's Diary Notes

Prayer for Today

Verse for Today

My reflections on today's verse

What Inspired Me Today

What have I been mindful of today?

Dear Lord, teach me to be

Dear Lord, share your light on

Dear Lord, hear my prayers for

Today I was grateful for...

Today I was encouraged by...

Today I saw God's hand in...

Today's Diary Notes

Prayer for Today

Verse for Today

My reflections on today's verse

What Inspired Me Today

What have I been mindful of today?

Dear Lord, teach me to be

| |
| |
| |
| |

Dear Lord, share your light on

| |
| |
| |
| |

Dear Lord, hear my prayers for

| |
| |
| |
| |

Today I was grateful for...

Today I was encouraged by...

Today I saw God's hand in...

Today's Diary Notes

Prayer for Today

Verse for Today

My reflections on today's verse

What Inspired Me Today

What have I been mindful of today?

Dear Lord, teach me to be

_____

_____

_____

_____

Dear Lord, share your light on

_____

_____

_____

_____

Dear Lord, hear my prayers for

_____

_____

_____

_____

Today I was grateful for...

Today I was encouraged by...

Today I saw God's hand in...

Today's Diary Notes

Prayer for Today

Verse for Today

My reflections on today's verse

What Inspired Me Today

What have I been mindful of today?

Dear Lord, teach me to be

_____

_____

_____

_____

Dear Lord, share your light on

_____

_____

_____

_____

Dear Lord, hear my prayers for

_____

_____

_____

_____

Today I was grateful for...

Today I was encouraged by...

Today I saw God's hand in...

Today's Diary Notes

Prayer for Today

Verse for Today

My reflections on today's verse

What Inspired Me Today

What have I been mindful of today?

Dear Lord, teach me to be

_____

_____

_____

_____

Dear Lord, share your light on

_____

_____

_____

_____

Dear Lord, hear my prayers for

_____

_____

_____

_____

Today I was grateful for...

Today I was encouraged by...

Today I saw God's hand in...

Today's Diary Notes

Prayer for Today

Verse for Today

My reflections on today's verse

What Inspired Me Today

What have I been mindful of today?

Dear Lord, teach me to be

_____

_____

_____

_____

Dear Lord, share your light on

_____

_____

_____

_____

Dear Lord, hear my prayers for

_____

_____

_____

_____

Today I was grateful for...

Today I was encouraged by...

Today I saw God's hand in...

Today's Diary Notes

Prayer for Today

Verse for Today

My reflections on today's verse

What Inspired Me Today

What have I been mindful of today?

Dear Lord, teach me to be

Dear Lord, share your light on

Dear Lord, hear my prayers for

Today I was grateful for...

Today I was encouraged by...

Today I saw God's hand in...

Today's Diary Notes

Prayer for Today

Verse for Today

My reflections on today's verse

What Inspired Me Today

What have I been mindful of today?

Dear Lord, teach me to be

_____

_____

_____

_____

Dear Lord, share your light on

_____

_____

_____

_____

Dear Lord, hear my prayers for

_____

_____

_____

_____

Today I was grateful for...

Today I was encouraged by...

Today I saw God's hand in...

Today's Diary Notes

Prayer for Today

Verse for Today

My reflections on today's verse

What Inspired Me Today

What have I been mindful of today?

Dear Lord, teach me to be

_____

Dear Lord, share your light on

_____

Dear Lord, hear my prayers for

_____

Today I was grateful for...

Today I was encouraged by...

Today I saw God's hand in...

Today's Diary Notes

Prayer for Today

Verse for Today

My reflections on today's verse

What Inspired Me Today

What have I been mindful of today?

Dear Lord, teach me to be

_____
_____
_____
_____

Dear Lord, share your light on

_____
_____
_____
_____

Dear Lord, hear my prayers for

_____
_____
_____
_____

Today I was grateful for...

Today I was encouraged by...

Today I saw God's hand in...

Today's Diary Notes

Prayer for Today

Verse for Today

My reflections on today's verse

What Inspired Me Today

What have I been mindful of today?

Dear Lord, teach me to be

_____

_____

_____

_____

Dear Lord, share your light on

_____

_____

_____

_____

Dear Lord, hear my prayers for

_____

_____

_____

_____

Today I was grateful for...

Today I was encouraged by...

Today I saw God's hand in...

Today's Diary Notes

Prayer for Today

Verse for Today

My reflections on today's verse

What Inspired Me Today

What have I been mindful of today?

Dear Lord, teach me to be

_____

_____

_____

_____

Dear Lord, share your light on

_____

_____

_____

_____

Dear Lord, hear my prayers for

_____

_____

_____

_____

Today I was grateful for...

Today I was encouraged by...

Today I saw God's hand in...

Today's Diary Notes

Prayer for Today

Verse for Today

My reflections on today's verse

What Inspired Me Today

What have I been mindful of today?

Dear Lord, teach me to be

Dear Lord, share your light on

Dear Lord, hear my prayers for

Today I was grateful for...

Today I was encouraged by...

Today I saw God's hand in...

Today's Diary Notes

Prayer for Today

Verse for Today

My reflections on today's verse

What Inspired Me Today

What have I been mindful of today?

Dear Lord, teach me to be

Dear Lord, share your light on

Dear Lord, hear my prayers for

Today I was grateful for...

Today I was encouraged by...

Today I saw God's hand in...

Today's Diary Notes

Prayer for Today

Verse for Today

My reflections on today's verse

What Inspired Me Today

What have I been mindful of today?

Dear Lord, teach me to be

| |
| |
| |
| |

Dear Lord, share your light on

| |
| |
| |
| |

Dear Lord, hear my prayers for

| |
| |
| |
| |

Today I was grateful for...

Today I was encouraged by...

Today I saw God's hand in...

Today's Diary Notes

Prayer for Today

Verse for Today

My reflections on today's verse

What Inspired Me Today

What have I been mindful of today?

Dear Lord, teach me to be

| |
| |
| |
| |

Dear Lord, share your light on

| |
| |
| |
| |

Dear Lord, hear my prayers for

| |
| |
| |
| |

Today I was grateful for...

Today I was encouraged by...

Today I saw God's hand in...

Today's Diary Notes

Prayer for Today

Verse for Today

My reflections on today's verse

What Inspired Me Today

What have I been mindful of today?

Dear Lord, teach me to be

_____
_____
_____
_____

Dear Lord, share your light on

_____
_____
_____
_____

Dear Lord, hear my prayers for

_____
_____
_____
_____

Today I was grateful for...

Today I was encouraged by...

Today I saw God's hand in...

Today's Diary Notes

Prayer for Today

Verse for Today

My reflections on today's verse

What Inspired Me Today

What have I been mindful of today?

Dear Lord, teach me to be

_____

_____

_____

_____

Dear Lord, share your light on

_____

_____

_____

_____

Dear Lord, hear my prayers for

_____

_____

_____

_____

Today I was grateful for...

Today I was encouraged by...

Today I saw God's hand in...

Today's Diary Notes

Prayer for Today

Verse for Today

My reflections on today's verse

What Inspired Me Today

What have I been mindful of today?

Dear Lord, teach me to be

_____

_____

_____

_____

Dear Lord, share your light on

_____

_____

_____

_____

Dear Lord, hear my prayers for

_____

_____

_____

_____

Today I was grateful for...

Today I was encouraged by...

Today I saw God's hand in...

Today's Diary Notes

Prayer for Today

Verse for Today

My reflections on today's verse

What Inspired Me Today

What have I been mindful of today?

Dear Lord, teach me to be

_____

_____

_____

_____

Dear Lord, share your light on

_____

_____

_____

_____

Dear Lord, hear my prayers for

_____

_____

_____

_____

Today I was grateful for...

Today I was encouraged by...

Today I saw God's hand in...

Today's Diary Notes

Prayer for Today

Verse for Today

My reflections on today's verse

What Inspired Me Today

What have I been mindful of today?

Dear Lord, teach me to be

_____

_____

_____

_____

Dear Lord, share your light on

_____

_____

_____

_____

Dear Lord, hear my prayers for

_____

_____

_____

_____

Today I was grateful for…

Today I was encouraged by…

Today I saw God's hand in…

Today's Diary Notes

Prayer for Today

Verse for Today

My reflections on today's verse

What Inspired Me Today

What have I been mindful of today?

Dear Lord, teach me to be

Dear Lord, share your light on

Dear Lord, hear my prayers for

Today I was grateful for...

Today I was encouraged by...

Today I saw God's hand in...

Today's Diary Notes

Prayer for Today

Verse for Today

My reflections on today's verse

What Inspired Me Today

What have I been mindful of today?

Dear Lord, teach me to be

| |
| |
| |
| |

Dear Lord, share your light on

| |
| |
| |
| |

Dear Lord, hear my prayers for

| |
| |
| |
| |

Today I was grateful for...

Today I was encouraged by...

Today I saw God's hand in...

Today's Diary Notes

Prayer for Today

Verse for Today

My reflections on today's verse

What Inspired Me Today

What have I been mindful of today?

Dear Lord, teach me to be

Dear Lord, share your light on

Dear Lord, hear my prayers for

Today I was grateful for...

Today I was encouraged by...

Today I saw God's hand in...

Today's Diary Notes

Prayer for Today

Verse for Today

My reflections on today's verse

What Inspired Me Today

What have I been mindful of today?

Dear Lord, teach me to be

Dear Lord, share your light on

Dear Lord, hear my prayers for

Today I was grateful for...

Today I was encouraged by...

Today I saw God's hand in...

Today's Diary Notes

Printed in Great Britain
by Amazon

54489431R00206